23260

23260

DATE DUE

First Facts™

Learning about Money

Scarcity

by Janeen R. Adil

Consultant:
Sharon M. Danes, PhD
Professor and Family Economist
University of Minnesota

Capstone press
Mankato, Minnesota

First Facts is published by Capstone Press,
151 Good Counsel Drive, P.O. Box 669, Mankato, Minnesota 56002.
www.capstonepress.com

Library of Congress Cataloging-in-Publication Data
Adil, Janeen R.
    Scarcity / by Janeen R. Adil.
    p. cm. — (First facts. Learning about money)
    Summary: "Introduces the economic principle of scarcity. Explains how scarcity affects prices
and choices. Includes an activity and fun facts"—Provided by publisher.
    Includes bibliographical references and index.
    ISBN-13: 978-0-7368-5399-6 (hardcover)
    ISBN-10: 0-7368-5399-5 (hardcover)
    1. Scarcity—Juvenile literature. 2. Natural resources—Juvenile literature. 3. Supply and
demand—Juvenile literature. 4. Consumption (Economics)—Juvenile literature. I. Title. II. Series.
HC85.A35 2006
338.5'21—dc22   2005021682

Editorial Credits
Wendy Dieker, editor; Jennifer Bergstrom, set designer; Bobbi J. Dey, book designer;
    Jo Miller, photo researcher/photo editor

Photo Credits
Capstone Press/Karon Dubke, cover, 5, 16–17, 19, 21
Corbis/Owen Franken, 20
David R. Frazier Photolibrary, 8–9, 10–11
Getty Images Inc./Joshua Rodas, 7
Superstock Inc., 6
Unicorn Stock Photos/Nancy Ferguson, 13; Tom McCarthy, 15

1 2 3 4 5 6 11 10 09 08 07 06

Table of Contents

What Is Scarcity?

These three girls each want an orange. But only one orange is left. Not all the girls can get what they want.

Things people want and use are **resources**. Just like these girls, people want more resources than they can have. There aren't enough resources for everyone. This is called scarcity.

Fact!
All countries, rich and poor, have scarcity. No country has enough resources for everything it wants.

How Scarcity Happens

All resources can be **scarce**. But some resources become more scarce at times. For example, cold weather can harm orange trees.

Then farmers have fewer oranges to pick and sell. Oranges would become scarce. There wouldn't be enough oranges for everyone.

When There Isn't Enough

What happens when oranges are scarce? Then a food **company** must choose how to use them. The company could make orange juice. Or it could just sell fresh oranges. The company might not be able to do both.

Fact!

In 2004, four hurricanes in Florida harmed many fruit trees. Farmers had fewer fruits to pick and sell during 2005.

Making Trade-offs

A food company might **decide** to sell just fresh oranges. That means it's also deciding not to sell juice. The company is making a **trade-off**. To sell only fresh oranges, it must give something up. The company gives up selling orange juice.

Prices

If oranges are scarce, not everyone can have them. But many people still want to buy oranges.

Stores raise the **prices** of scarce items. Oranges cost more money when they are scarce. If people want the oranges, they must pay a higher price.

Fact!
Orange prices were low before the 2004 Florida hurricanes damaged orange trees. After the hurricanes, the prices went up because oranges were scarce.

Making Choices

Scarcity means people have to make choices at the store. If oranges are scarce, what are the choices? People can pay a higher price for the oranges. They can also try to find a better price at a different store. Or they could buy another fruit instead.

A Scarce Toy

Just like oranges, toys can be scarce. Ben wants to buy his sister a popular toy for her birthday. But the store near their house has sold out. The toy has become scarce.

Ben Must Choose

Ben looks at other stores around town. At last he finds the toy. But this store is charging a high price.

Now Ben has to make a choice. Should he buy the toy at this high price? Should he keep looking for a better price? Or should he buy his sister something else? What would you do?

Fact!
In 1993, the first Beanie Babies sold for just a few dollars. The kinds that aren't made anymore are scarce. People pay hundreds of dollars for these toys!

Cars can't run without gas. In the 1970s, though, there wasn't enough gas. People waited in long lines for hours to fill up their cars. Not everyone who wanted gas could buy it. Some people stopped driving. Instead, they walked, rode bikes, or took the train.

Hands On: Some More S'mores

Scarcity forces us to make choices. We don't always have enough resources to make everything we want. Do this activity with a friend to see how a scarce item forces you to make choices.

What You Need

3 marshmallows
12 graham cracker squares
3 milk chocolate candy bars

What You Do

1. Make a s'more sandwich. Layer 1 cracker, ½ a chocolate bar, and 1 marshmallow. Top with another cracker.
2. Using only the items listed above, make 5 more sandwiches for you and your friend to share.

Which item is scarce? Can you make all 6 sandwiches as instructed? What are your choices?

Glossary

company (KUM-pan-ee)—a business that buys resources and decides how to use and sell them

decide (di-SIDE)—to make up your mind about something

price (PRISSE)—how much money a person pays for something

resource (REE-sorss)—something useful to a place or person

scarce (SKAIRSS)—being hard to find because there's very little of it

trade-off (TRADE-off)—the giving up of one thing for another

Read More

Adil, Janeen R. *Supply and Demand.* Learning about Money. Mankato, Minn: Capstone Press, 2006.

Berenstain, Stan, and Jan Berenstain. *The Berenstain Bears' Mad, Mad, Mad Toy Craze.* First Time Books. New York: Random House, 1999.

Internet Sites

FactHound offers a safe, fun way to find Internet sites related to this book. All of the sites on FactHound have been researched by our staff.

Here's how:
1. Visit *www.facthound.com*
2. Type in this special code **0736853995** for age-appropriate sites. Or enter a search word related to this book for a more general search.
3. Click on the **Fetch It** button.

FactHound will fetch the best sites for you!

Index